SCHOLASTIC

W9-BAE-968

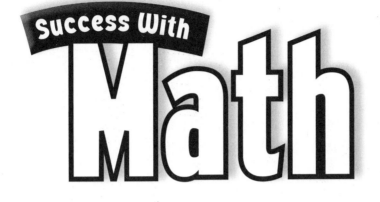

Success With

Math

New York • Toronto • London • Auckland • Sydney
Mexico City • New Delhi • Hong Kong • Buenos Aires

Teaching
Resources

State Standards Correlations

To find out how this book helps you meet your state's standards,
log on to **www.scholastic.com/ssw**

Scholastic Inc. grants teachers permission to photocopy the reproducible pages from this book for classroom use.
No other part of this publication may be reproduced in whole or in part, or stored in a retrieval system,
or transmitted in any form or by any means, electronic, mechanical, photocopying, recording,
or otherwise without written permission of the publisher. For information regarding permission,
write to Scholastic Inc., 557 Broadway, New York, NY 10012.

Cover design by Ka-Yeon Kim-Li
Interior design by Ellen Matlach Hassell
for Boultinghouse & Boultinghouse, Inc.

ISBN 978-0-545-20070-7

Copyright © 2002, 2010 Scholastic Inc.
All rights reserved. Printed in the U.S.A.

26 27   40   21 20

Contents

About the Book

"Nothing succeeds like success."
—Alexandre Dumas the Elder, 1854

And no other math resource helps kids succeed like *Scholastic Success With Math!* For classroom or at-home use, this exciting series for kids in grades 1 through 5 provides invaluable reinforcement and practice for math skills such as:

- ❏ number sense and concepts
- ❏ reasoning and logic
- ❏ basic operations and computations
- ❏ story problems and equations
- ❏ time, money, and measurement
- ❏ fractions, decimals, and percentages
- ❏ geometry and basic shapes
- ❏ graphs, charts, tables ... and more!

This 64-page book contains loads of challenging puzzles, inviting games, and clever practice pages to keep kids delighted and excited as they strengthen their basic math skills.

What makes *Scholastic Success With Math* so solid?

Each practice page reinforces a specific, age-appropriate skill as outlined in one or more standardized tests. These are the skills that help kids succeed in daily math work and on standardized achievement tests. And the handy Instant Skills Index at the back of the book helps you succeed in zeroing in on the skills your kids need most!

Take the lead and help kids succeed with *Scholastic Success With Math*.
Parents and teachers agree: No one helps kids succeed like Scholastic!

Lone Donor

Name _____ Date _____

This is a number line. The numbers increase as you go along the line.

Write the missing numbers.

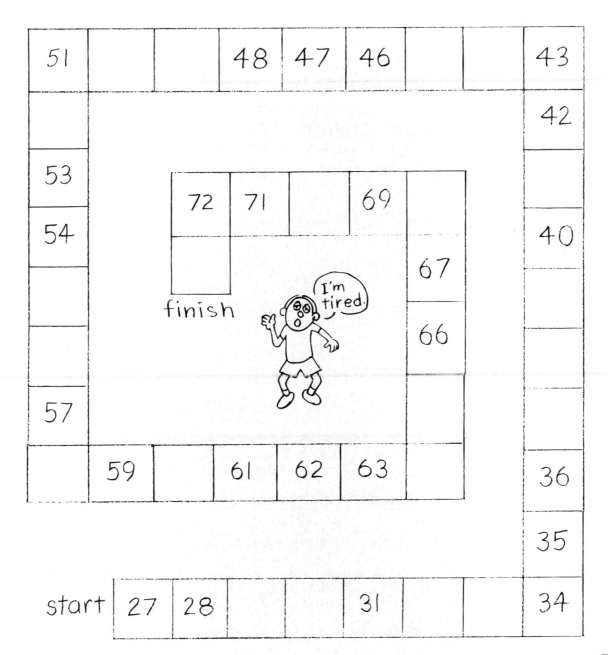

Copyright © Scholastic Inc.

5

Mystery Critter

Name _____ Date _____

I climb up the side of walls and never fall.

I am a fast runner and have a very long tail. Who am I? _____

To find out, connect the numbers in order from 20 to 68.

Order Recorder

Name _____ Date _____

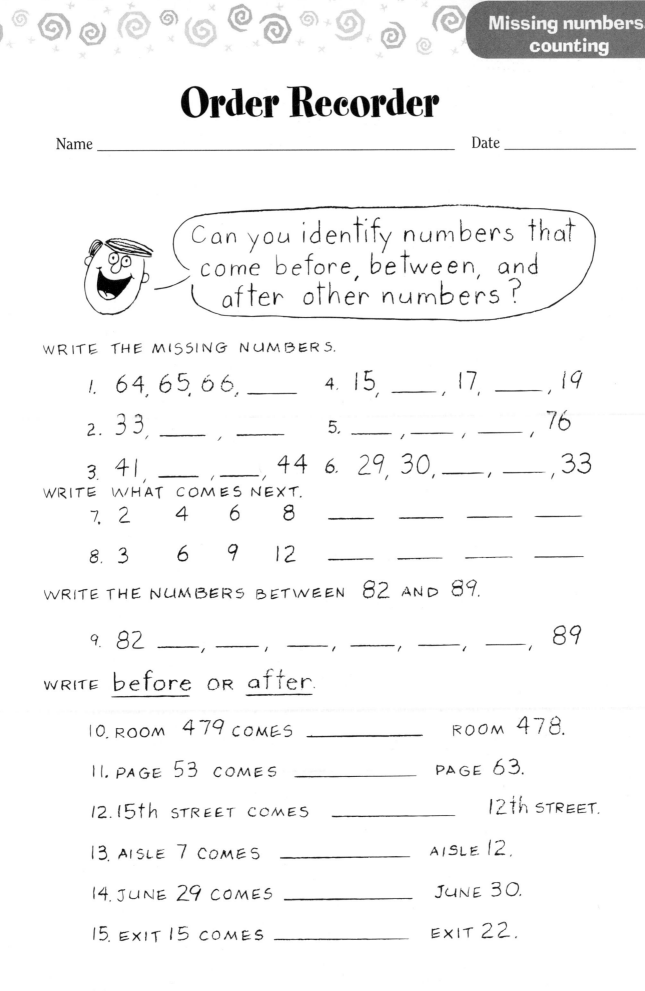

Can you identify numbers that come before, between, and after other numbers?

WRITE THE MISSING NUMBERS.

1. 64, 65, 66, ____

2. 33, ____ , ____

3. 41, ____ , ____ , 44

4. 15, ____ , 17, ____ , 19

5. ____ , ____ , ____ , 76

6. 29, 30, ____ , ____ , 33

WRITE WHAT COMES NEXT.

7. 2   4   6   8   ____ ____ ____ ____

8. 3   6   9   12   ____ ____ ____ ____

WRITE THE NUMBERS BETWEEN 82 AND 89.

9. 82 ____ , ____ , ____ , ____ , ____ , ____ , 89

WRITE before OR after.

10. ROOM 479 COMES _____ ROOM 478.

11. PAGE 53 COMES _____ PAGE 63.

12. 15th STREET COMES _____ 12th STREET.

13. AISLE 7 COMES _____ AISLE 12.

14. JUNE 29 COMES _____ JUNE 30.

15. EXIT 15 COMES _____ EXIT 22.

Copyright © Scholastic Inc.

Missing Bone

Name _____ Date _____

McAllister the Mutt is dog-tired from walking in circles trying to find his bone. To help him find the path to the bone, move one paw print at a time in any direction except diagonally. You can only follow the tracks that have odd numbers. Draw a line to show his route.

Patterns for the Mail Carrier

Name _____ Date _____

Meimei the mail carrier is delivering letters. Give her some help. Fill in the missing addresses on the houses below.

Extra

What pattern do you see in the house numbers? _____

_____

_____

_____

Copyright © Scholastic Inc.

9

Presidents' Day Problem

Name _____ Date _____

The first 18 Presidents of the United States are listed below.
They are shown in order.

1. George Washington (1789–1797)	2. John Adams (1797–1801)	3. Thomas Jefferson (1801–1809)
4. James Madison (1809–1817)	5. James Monroe (1817–1825)	6. John Quincy Adams (1825 1829)
7. Andrew Jackson (1829–1837)	8. Martin Van Buren (1837–1841)	9. William Henry Harrison (1841)
10. John Tyler (1841–1845)	11. James Knox Polk (1845–1849)	12. Zachary Taylor (1849–1850)
13. Millard Fillmore (1850–1853)	14. Franklin Pierce (1853–1857)	15. James Buchanan (1857–1861)
16. Abraham Lincoln (1861–1865)	17. Andrew Johnson (1865–1869)	18. Ulysses S. Grant (1869–1877)

1. Which President was Washington? _____ **the 1st** _____

2. Which President was Lincoln? _____

3. Which President came before Lincoln? _____

4. Which President came after Lincoln? _____

5. How many Presidents were there
   <u>between</u> Washington and Lincoln? _____

Amused Chooser

Name _____ Date _____

Compare numbers: > means "greater than." < means "less than." = means "equal to" or "same as." Hint: The arrow points to the number that is less.

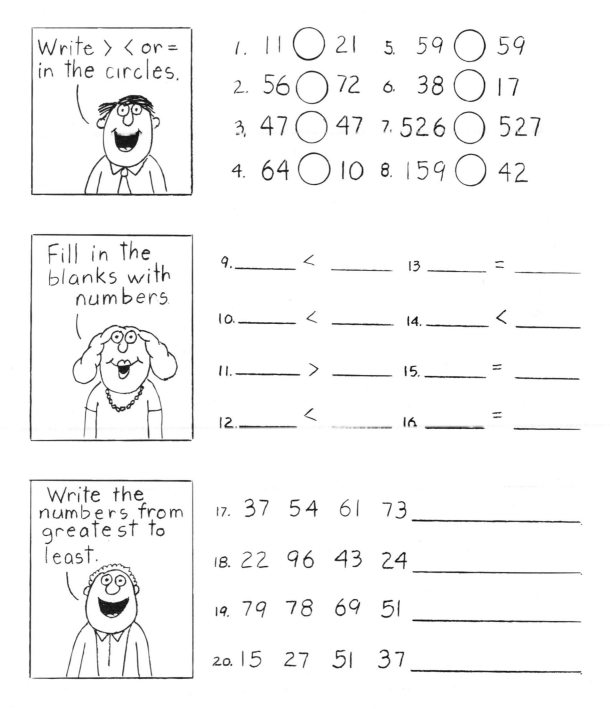

Write > < or = in the circles.

1. 11 ◯ 21   5. 59 ◯ 59
2. 56 ◯ 72   6. 38 ◯ 17
3. 47 ◯ 47   7. 526 ◯ 527
4. 64 ◯ 10   8. 159 ◯ 42

Fill in the blanks with numbers.

9. _____ < _____   13. _____ = _____
10. _____ < _____   14. _____ < _____
11. _____ > _____   15. _____ = _____
12. _____ < _____   16. _____ = _____

Write the numbers from greatest to least.

17. 37 54 61 73 _____

18. 22 96 43 24 _____

19. 79 78 69 51 _____

20. 15 27 51 37 _____

Copyright © Scholastic Inc.

Riddle Fun

Name _____ Date _____

What wears shoes, sandals, and boots, but has no feet?

A ___ ___ ___ ___ ___ ___ ___ ___

To find out, write each number in standard form. Then look for the numbers in the puzzle and circle them. They are written up, down, and backward. When you have circled all the numbers given, the letters in the blocks left uncircled spell the answer to the riddle. The first number has been circled for you.

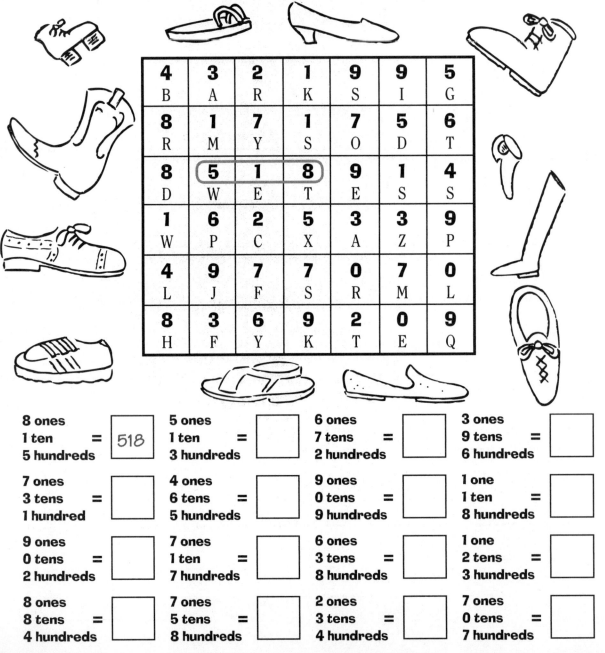

4	3	2	1	9	9	5
B	A	R	K	S	I	G
8	1	7	1	7	5	6
R	M	Y	S	O	D	T
8	5	1	8	9	1	4
D	W	E	T	E	S	S
1	6	2	5	3	3	9
W	P	C	X	A	Z	P
4	9	7	7	0	7	0
L	J	F	S	R	M	L
8	3	6	9	2	0	9
H	F	Y	K	T	E	Q

8 ones
1 ten   = 518
5 hundreds

5 ones
1 ten   =
3 hundreds

6 ones
7 tens   =
2 hundreds

3 ones
9 tens   =
6 hundreds

7 ones
3 tens   =
1 hundred

4 ones
6 tens   =
5 hundreds

9 ones
0 tens   =
9 hundreds

1 one
1 ten   =
8 hundreds

9 ones
0 tens   =
2 hundreds

7 ones
1 ten   =
7 hundreds

6 ones
3 tens   =
8 hundreds

1 one
2 tens   =
3 hundreds

8 ones
8 tens   =
4 hundreds

7 ones
5 tens   =
8 hundreds

2 ones
3 tens   =
4 hundreds

7 ones
0 tens   =
7 hundreds

Pattern Learner

Name _____ Date _____

A pattern is a repeated arrangement of numbers, shapes, or lines in a
row. Continue the patterns below.

1. 324, 435, 546, _____, _____, _____

2. ▢ ◯ △ ▢ ◯ _____

3. _____

4. _____

5. _____

6. _____

7. A C E G I K _____

8. 11:05, 11:10, 11:15, _____, _____

9. _____

Copyright © Scholastic Inc.

13

Shape Tricks

Name _____ Date _____

Danny's class was learning about shapes. He noticed that you could draw a line across one shape to make two shapes. Draw a line through each shape below to make two new shapes. (Pattern blocks may help you.)

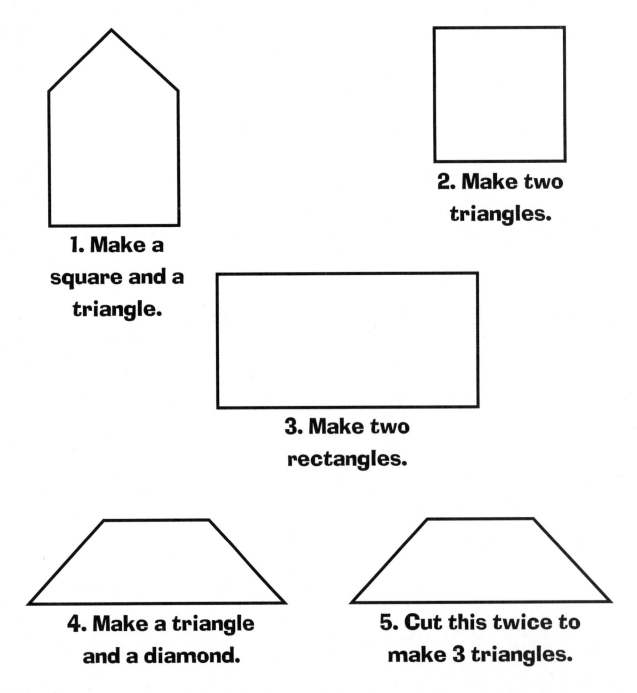

1. Make a square and a triangle.

2. Make two triangles.

3. Make two rectangles.

4. Make a triangle and a diamond.

5. Cut this twice to make 3 triangles.

Picking Out Patterns

Name _____ Date _____

On the 100th day of school, everyone in Pat's class picked out patterns on the 100 Chart. Look at the chart below.

1	2	3	4	5	6	7	8	9	10
11	12	13	14	15	16	17	18	19	20
21	22	23	24	25	26	27	28	29	30
31	32	33	34	35	36	37	38	39	40
41	42	43	44	45	46	47	48	49	50
51	52	53	54	55	56	57	58	59	60
61	62	63	64	65	66	67	68	69	70
71	72	73	74	75	76	77	78	79	80
81	82	83	84	85	86	87	88	89	90
91	92	93	94	95	96	97	98	99	100

Find and finish the pattern starting with 2, 12, 22

_____

Find and finish the pattern starting with 100, 90, 80

_____

Find and finish the pattern starting with 97, 87, 77

_____

Find and finish the pattern starting with 11, 22, 33

_____

Copyright © Scholastic Inc.

Shape Study

Name _____ Date _____

A heptagon has 7 sides. On a heptagon, all the sides are the same length.

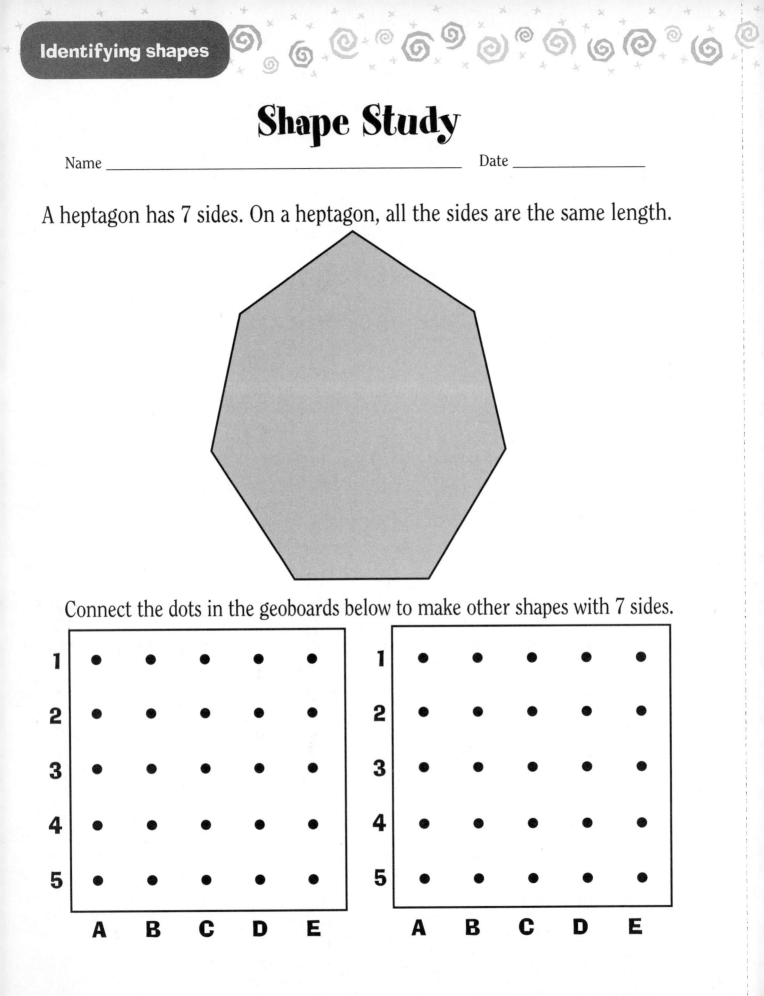

Connect the dots in the geoboards below to make other shapes with 7 sides.

Shape Gaper

Name _____ Date _____

FLAT SHAPES HAVE LENGTH AND WIDTH.

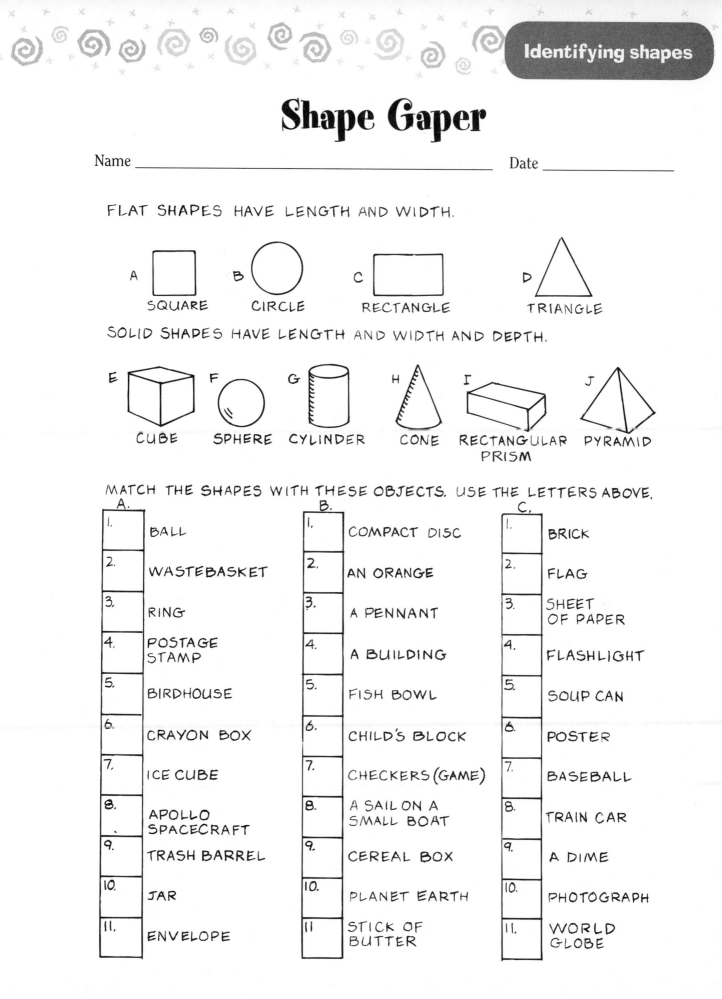

A SQUARE   B CIRCLE   C RECTANGLE   D TRIANGLE

SOLID SHAPES HAVE LENGTH AND WIDTH AND DEPTH.

E CUBE   F SPHERE   G CYLINDER   H CONE   I RECTANGULAR PRISM   J PYRAMID

MATCH THE SHAPES WITH THESE OBJECTS. USE THE LETTERS ABOVE.

A.
1.	BALL
2.	WASTEBASKET
3.	RING
4.	POSTAGE STAMP
5.	BIRDHOUSE
6.	CRAYON BOX
7.	ICE CUBE
8.	APOLLO SPACECRAFT
9.	TRASH BARREL
10.	JAR
11.	ENVELOPE

B.
1.	COMPACT DISC
2.	AN ORANGE
3.	A PENNANT
4.	A BUILDING
5.	FISH BOWL
6.	CHILD'S BLOCK
7.	CHECKERS (GAME)
8.	A SAIL ON A SMALL BOAT
9.	CEREAL BOX
10.	PLANET EARTH
11	STICK OF BUTTER

C.
1.	BRICK
2.	FLAG
3.	SHEET OF PAPER
4.	FLASHLIGHT
5.	SOUP CAN
6.	POSTER
7.	BASEBALL
8.	TRAIN CAR
9.	A DIME
10.	PHOTOGRAPH
11.	WORLD GLOBE

Copyright © Scholastic Inc.

Scarecrow Sam

Name _____ Date _____

Why doesn't Scarecrow Sam tell secrets when he is near Farmer Joe's bean patch? _____

To find out the answer, add the numbers. Circle the pumpkins that have sums of 14, and write the letters that appear inside those pumpkins in order in the boxes below.

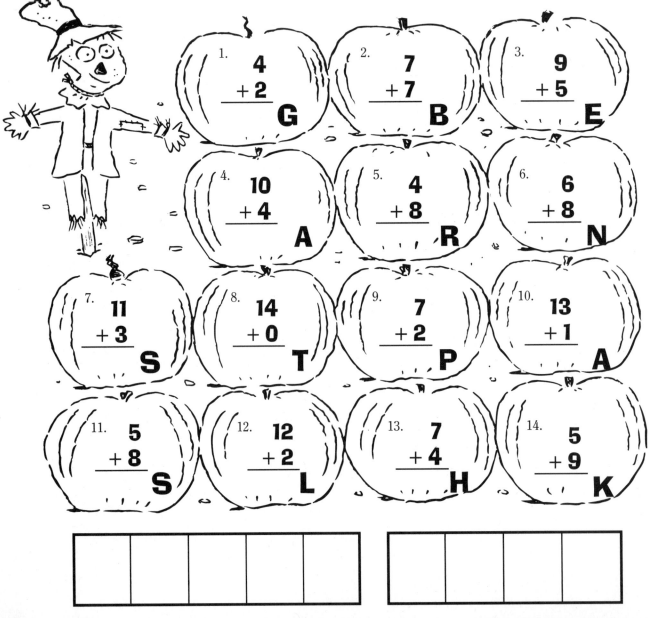

1. 4
   + 2
     G

2. 7
   + 7
     B

3. 9
   + 5
     E

4. 10
   + 4
     A

5. 4
   + 8
     R

6. 6
   + 8
     N

7. 11
   + 3
     S

8. 14
   + 0
     T

9. 7
   + 2
     P

10. 13
    + 1
      A

11. 5
    + 8
      S

12. 12
    + 2
      L

13. 7
    + 4
      H

14. 5
    + 9
      K

Crossdigit Wiz

Name _____ Date _____

Find the sums of the three addends in the rows across and down. The answer circles are numbered.

Copyright © Scholastic Inc.

You've Got Mail!

Name _____ Date _____

1. Solve the problems.
2. Find each number pair on the graph. Make a dot for each.
3. Connect the dots in the order that you make them.
4. What picture did you make?

_____

	Across	**Up**
1.	20 + 7 = _____	12 + 12 = _____
2.	12 + 3 = _____	11 + 13 = _____
3.	1 + 2 = _____	10 + 14 = _____
4.	13 + 2 = _____	10 + 5 = _____
5.	13 + 14 = _____	21 + 3 = _____
6.	23 + 4 = _____	11 + 4 = _____
7.	5 + 22 = _____	2 + 4 = _____
8.	3 + 12 = _____	1 + 5 = _____
9.	3 + 0 = _____	6 + 0 = _____
10.	2 + 1 = _____	2 + 13 = _____
11.	0 + 3 = _____	2 + 22 = _____

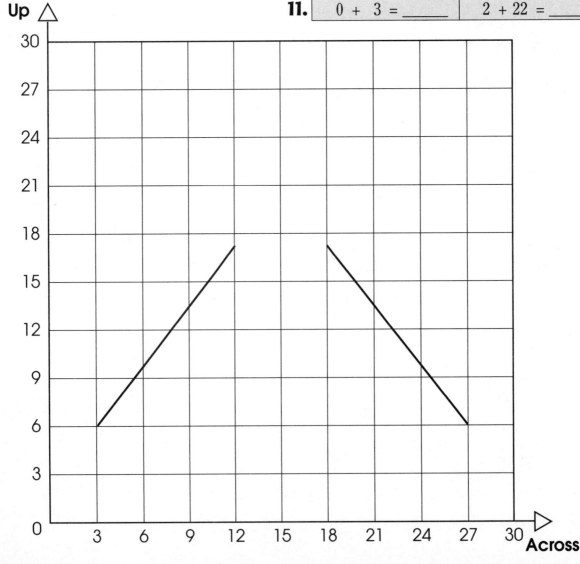

Up

Across

Kaleidoscope

Name _____ Date _____

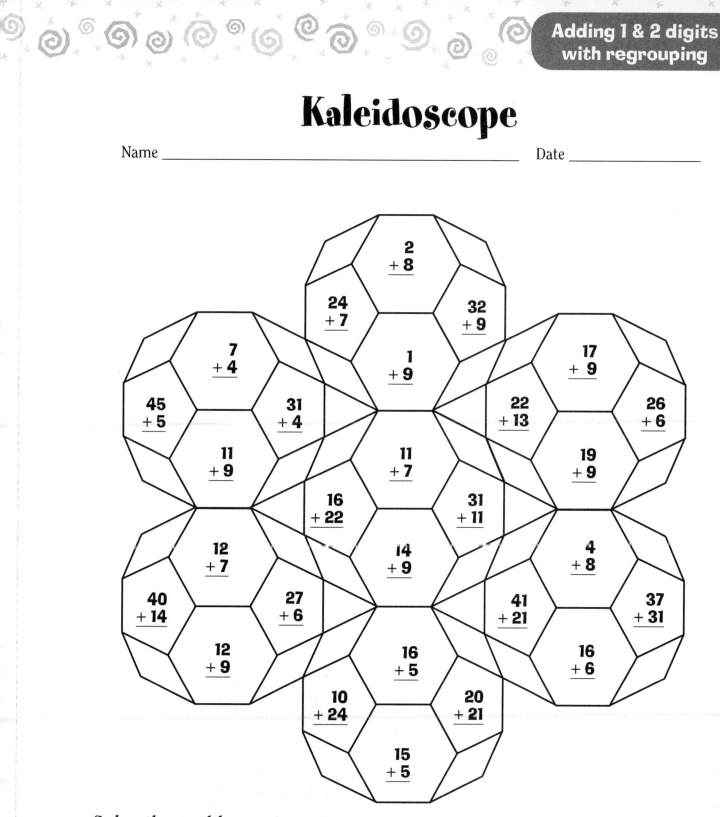

Solve the problems.

If the answer is between 1 and 30, color the shape red.

If the answer is between 31 and 99, color the shape gray.

Finish by coloring the other shapes with the colors of your choice.

Extra: Name two numbers that when added together equal 27.

Copyright © Scholastic Inc.

Carnival Fun

Name _____ Date _____

Do the problems below. Then find your answers hidden in the carnival scene and circle them. Can you find all twelve answers?

$$\begin{array}{r} 15 \\ 33 \\ + 27 \\ \hline \end{array}$$
$$\begin{array}{r} 27 \\ 23 \\ + 12 \\ \hline \end{array}$$
$$\begin{array}{r} 34 \\ 23 \\ + 24 \\ \hline \end{array}$$
$$\begin{array}{r} 15 \\ 25 \\ + 10 \\ \hline \end{array}$$
$$\begin{array}{r} 16 \\ 14 \\ + 14 \\ \hline \end{array}$$
$$\begin{array}{r} 12 \\ 31 \\ + 17 \\ \hline \end{array}$$

$$\begin{array}{r} 28 \\ 22 \\ + 45 \\ \hline \end{array}$$
$$\begin{array}{r} 43 \\ 27 \\ + 27 \\ \hline \end{array}$$
$$\begin{array}{r} 10 \\ 17 \\ + 18 \\ \hline \end{array}$$
$$\begin{array}{r} 29 \\ 13 \\ + 16 \\ \hline \end{array}$$
$$\begin{array}{r} 37 \\ 31 \\ + 17 \\ \hline \end{array}$$
$$\begin{array}{r} 51 \\ 23 \\ + 17 \\ \hline \end{array}$$

Zoo Animal

Name _____ Date _____

1. Solve the problems.
2. Find each number pair on the graph. Make a dot for each.
3. Connect the dots in the order that you make them.
4. What picture did you make?

_____

	Across	Up		Across	Up
1.	13 + 7 = _____	12 + 4 = _____	**8.**	17 + 15 = _____	1 + 3 = _____
2.	15 + 9 = _____	5 + 3 = _____	**9.**	31 + 9 = _____	3 + 1 = _____
3.	11 + 9 = _____	0 + 4 = _____	**10.**	8 + 32 = _____	8 + 8 = _____
4.	19 + 9 = _____	2 + 2 = _____	**11.**	19 + 25 = _____	19 + 1 = _____
5.	10 + 18 = _____	11 + 5 = _____	**12.**	27 + 17 = _____	18 + 14 = _____
6.	16 + 16 = _____	9 + 7 = _____	**13.**	7 + 29 = _____	17 + 23 = _____
7.	28 + 8 = _____	2 + 6 = _____	**14.**	18 + 6 = _____	25 + 15 = _____

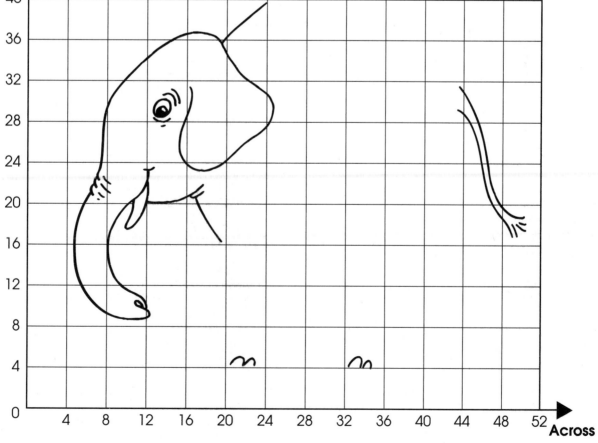

Copyright © Scholastic Inc.

Tricky Twins

Name _____ Date _____

Sandy and Mandy are having a twin party. There are six sets of twins, but only one set of identical twins. To find the identical twins, solve the addition problems under each person. The identical twins have the same answer.

207 + 545	126 + 89	328 + 347	257 + 458

547 +129	624 +127	108 +107	229 +418

258 + 268	389 + 336	417 + 129	253 + 494

Eager Leader

Name _____ Date _____

Fill in the missing numbers.

$$\begin{array}{r} 2\ \square\ 8 \\ +\ \square\ 5\ \square \\ \hline 6\ 7\ 9 \end{array}$$

$$\begin{array}{r} 4\ 0\ \square \\ +\ 3\ \square\ 5 \\ \hline \square\ 1\ 8 \end{array}$$

$$\begin{array}{r} 2\ \square\ 7 \\ +\ \square\ 5\ \square \\ \hline 3\ 9\ 8 \end{array}$$

$$\begin{array}{r} 3\ \square\ \square \\ +\ 1\ 2\ 4 \\ \hline \square\ 7\ 8 \end{array}$$

$$\begin{array}{r} 1\ 2\ 5 \\ +\ \square\ \square\ \square \\ \hline 4\ 7\ 9 \end{array}$$

$$\begin{array}{r} 1\ 5\ \square \\ +\ 3\ \square\ 2 \\ \hline \square\ 9\ 2 \end{array}$$

How are you doing?

$$\begin{array}{r} 5\ \square\ 8 \\ +\ \square\ 6\ \square \\ \hline 7\ 6\ 9 \end{array}$$

$$\begin{array}{r} 4\ \square\ \square \\ +\ 2\ 2\ 0 \\ \hline \square\ 7\ 9 \end{array}$$

$$\begin{array}{r} 1\ 4\ 6 \\ +\ \square\ 3\ \square \\ \hline 3\ \square\ 8 \end{array}$$

$$\begin{array}{r} 3\ 1\ 4 \\ +\ \square\ \square\ \square \\ \hline 4\ 3\ 7 \end{array}$$

Copyright © Scholastic Inc.

25

Eager Seeker

Name _____ Date _____

Divide the objects and food equally among the groups of people shown below. How many will each person receive? How much will be left over?

ITEM	NUMBER OF PEOPLE	EACH	LEFT OVER
1. 28 MARBLES			
2. 15 STICKS OF BUBBLE GUM			
3. 8 ONE DOLLAR BILLS			
4. 15 SLICES OF PIZZA			
5. 4 BALLOONS			
6. 25 MARSHMALLOWS			
7. 6 TOY DINOSAURS			
8. 29 FRENCH FRIES			
9. 12 STRAWBERRIES			
10. 19 COOKIES			

Time to Get Up!

Name _____ Date _____

Twenty animals were hibernating near Sleepy Pond.
5 of them woke up. Color 5 animals below.
How many are still sleeping? _____
A week later, 7 more woke up. Color 7 other animals.
How many are still sleeping? _____

Copyright © Scholastic Inc.

27

Detective Work

Name _____ Date _____

Use the code to help Detective Dave discover the secret phone number.
The first problem has been done for you.

1	2	3
4	5	6
7	8	9

1.

$7 - 1 = 6$

2.

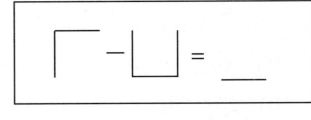

3.

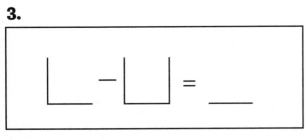

4.

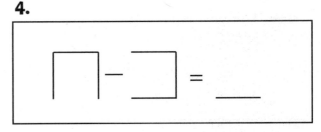

5.

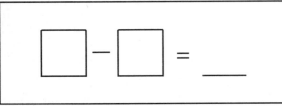

6.

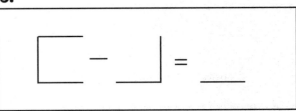

7.

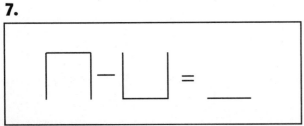

The phone number is:

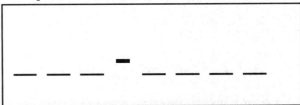
___ ___ ___ — ___ ___ ___ ___

Chirp, Chirp!

Name _____ Date _____

1. Solve the problems.
2. Find each number pair on the graph. Make a dot for each.
3. Connect the dots in the order that you make them.
4. What picture did you make?

_____

	Across	Up
1.	10 – 7 = _____	10 – 8 = _____
2.	4 – 2 = _____	3 – 1 = _____
3.	7 – 5 = _____	1 – 0 = _____
4.	8 – 0 = _____	1 – 0 = _____
5.	9 – 1 = _____	8 – 6 = _____
6.	10 – 3 = _____	7 – 5 = _____
7.	10 – 2 = _____	8 – 2 = _____
8.	8 – 3 = _____	10 – 0 = _____
9.	9 – 7 = _____	7 – 1 = _____
10.	4 – 1 = _____	5 – 3 = _____
11.	9 – 2 = _____	6 – 4 = _____

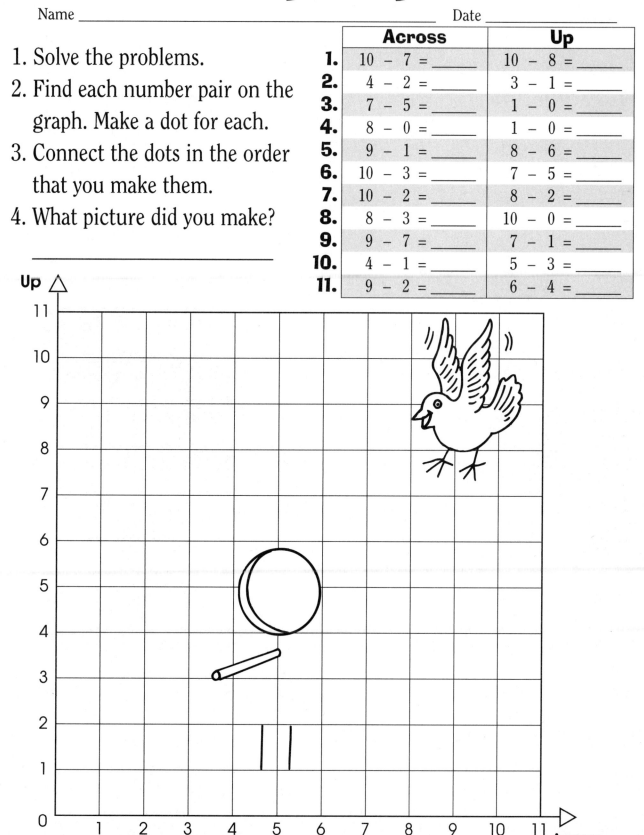

Copyright © Scholastic Inc.

Winter Is Coming

Name _____   Date _____

Do the subtraction problems. Help Mr. Squirrel find his way to the tree
where he is storing acorns for the winter. Make sure
he doesn't cross any odd answers.

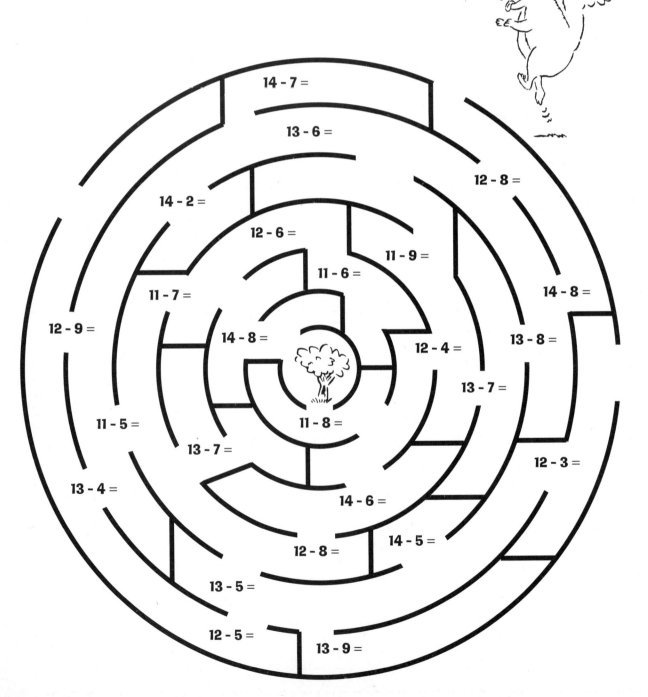

14 - 7 =

13 - 6 =

12 - 8 =

14 - 2 =

12 - 6 =

11 - 9 =

11 - 6 =

11 - 7 =

14 - 8 =

12 - 9 =

14 - 8 =

12 - 4 =

13 - 8 =

13 - 7 =

11 - 5 =

11 - 8 =

13 - 7 =

12 - 3 =

13 - 4 =

14 - 6 =

14 - 5 =

12 - 8 =

13 - 5 =

12 - 5 =

13 - 9 =

Baseball Puzzle

Name _____   Date _____

What animal can always be found at a baseball game?

_____

To find out, do the subtraction problems. If the answer is greater than 9, color the shapes black. If the answer is less than 10, color the shapes red.

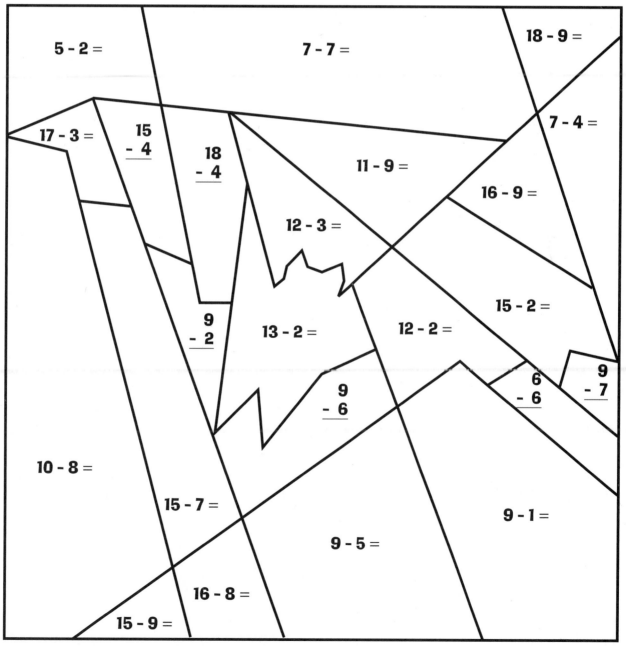

$5 - 2 =$

$7 - 7 =$

$18 - 9 =$

$17 - 3 =$

$\begin{array}{r} 15 \\ -\ 4 \\ \hline \end{array}$

$\begin{array}{r} 18 \\ -\ 4 \\ \hline \end{array}$

$11 - 9 =$

$7 - 4 =$

$16 - 9 =$

$12 - 3 =$

$\begin{array}{r} 9 \\ -\ 2 \\ \hline \end{array}$

$13 - 2 =$

$12 - 2 =$

$15 - 2 =$

$\begin{array}{r} 9 \\ -\ 6 \\ \hline \end{array}$

$\begin{array}{r} 6 \\ -\ 6 \\ \hline \end{array}$

$\begin{array}{r} 9 \\ -\ 7 \\ \hline \end{array}$

$10 - 8 =$

$15 - 7 =$

$9 - 1 =$

$9 - 5 =$

$16 - 8 =$

$15 - 9 =$

Copyright © Scholastic Inc.

Bubble Yum!

Name _____   Date _____

1. Solve the problems.
2. Find each number pair on the graph. Make a dot for each.
3. Connect the dots in the order that you make them.
4. What picture did you make?

_____

	Across	Up
1.	27 – 23 = _____	58 – 53 = _____
2.	18 – 15 = _____	23 – 21 = _____
3.	30 – 27 = _____	29 – 28 = _____
4.	18 – 11 = _____	46 – 45 = _____
5.	58 – 51 = _____	17 – 15 = _____
6.	28 – 22 = _____	49 – 44 = _____
7.	19 – 15 = _____	77 – 72 = _____

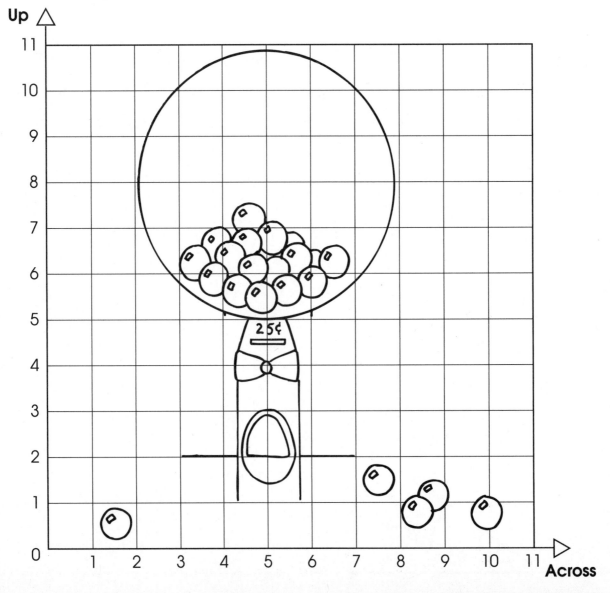

Scholastic Success With Math: Grade 2

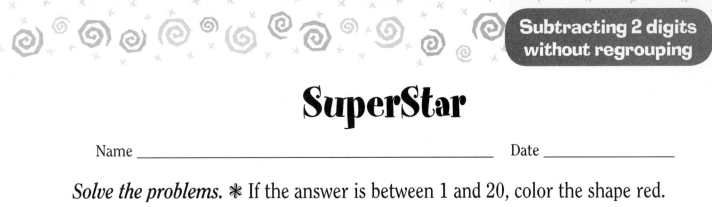

SuperStar

Name _____   Date _____

Solve the problems. ✳ If the answer is between 1 and 20, color the shape red. ✳ If the answer is between 21 and 40, color the shape white. ✳ If the answer is between 41 and 90, color the shape blue. ✳ *Taking It Further:* Write five subtraction problems that have answers between 10 and 20.

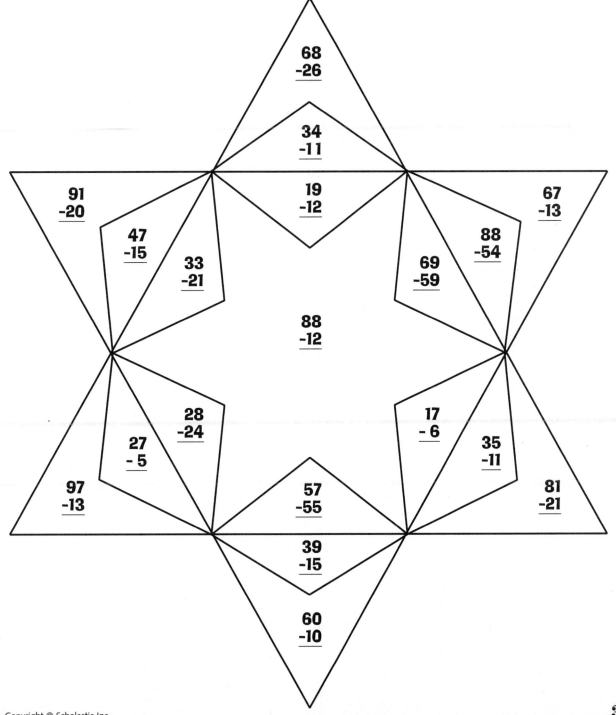

Copyright © Scholastic Inc.

Purdy Bird

Name _____   Date _____

Purdy the Parakeet loves to look at herself in the mirror. Only one of these parakeets below really shows what Purdy looks like in the mirror. Can you find the right one? To check your answer, do the subtraction problems next to each bird. The answer for the correct bird is 24.

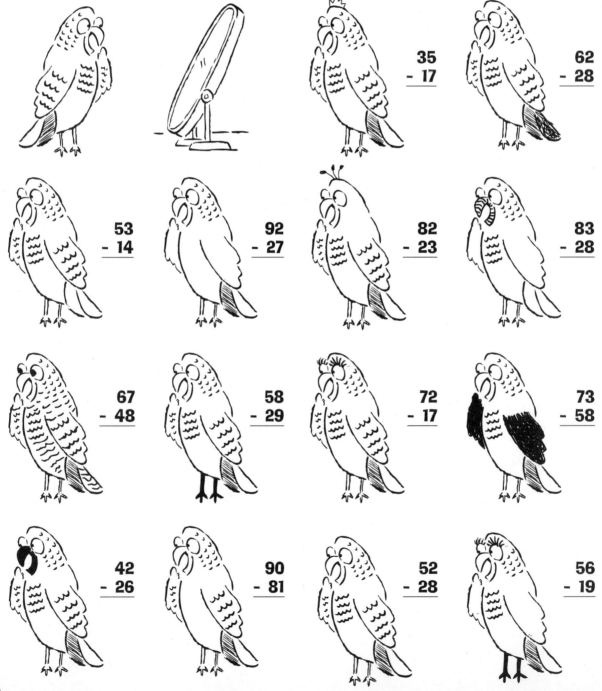

$$35 - 17$$

$$62 - 28$$

$$53 - 14$$

$$92 - 27$$

$$82 - 23$$

$$83 - 28$$

$$67 - 48$$

$$58 - 29$$

$$72 - 17$$

$$73 - 58$$

$$42 - 26$$

$$90 - 81$$

$$52 - 28$$

$$56 - 19$$

Grandma's Quilt

Name _____ Date _____

Solve the problems. ✳ If the answer is between 1 and 50, color the shape red. ✳ If the answer is between 51 and 100, color the shape blue. ✳ Finish the design by coloring the other shapes with the colors of your choice. ✳ *Taking It Further:* Amelia bought 30 tickets for rides at the carnival. She used 15 tickets in the first hour. How many tickets did she have left?

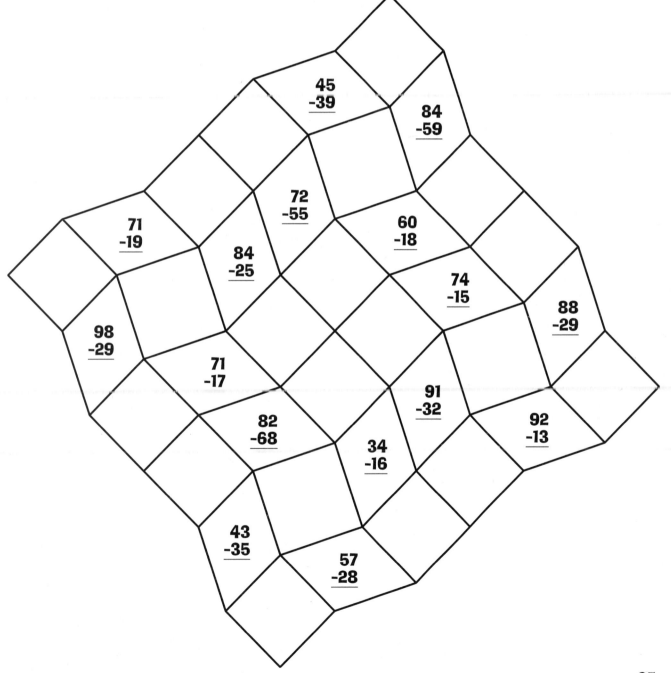

45
-39

84
-59

72
-55

71
-19

60
-18

84
-25

74
-15

88
-29

98
-29

71
-17

91
-32

92
-13

82
-68

34
-16

43
-35

57
-28

Copyright © Scholastic Inc.

Rocket Riddle

Name _____ Date _____

What did the rocket say
when it left the party?

What To Do

To find the answer to the riddle,
solve the multiplication problems.
Then match each product with a
letter in the Key below. Write the
correct letters on the blanks below.

1   **5 x 1** = _____   **6**   **5 x 2** = _____

2   **8 x 1** = _____   **7**   **6 x 2** = _____

3   **11 x 1** = _____   **8**   **8 x 2** = _____

4   **26 x 1** = _____   **9**   **9 x 2** = _____

5   **3 x 2** = _____   **10**   **12 x 2** = _____

Key

10 .... F	27 .... U	20 .... W
13 C	8 .... E	7 .... D
11 .... O	6 .... K	12 .... T
16 .... E	9 .... B	26 .... O
5 .... A	24 .... F	18 .... T

Riddle
Answer: "TIM ___   ___ ___   ___ ___ ___ ___   ___ ___ ___."
        8   **7** **3**   **9** **1** **5** **2**   **4** **6** **10**

Wise Owls

Name _____   Date _____

What did the owl say when
someone knocked on its door?

What To Do

To find the answer to the riddle,
solve the multiplication problems.
Then match each product with a
letter in the Key below. Write the
correct letters on the blanks below.

1 **5 x 3** = _____   **6** **6 x 3** = _____

2 **2 x 3** = _____   **7** **10 x 3** = _____

3 **8 x 3** = _____   **8** **12 x 3** = _____

4 **4 x 3** = _____   **9** **11 x 3** = _____

5 **9 x 3** = _____   **10** **0 x 3** = _____

Key

30	O	8	K	42	N
11	A	15	O	24	T
36	H	0	I	33	O
18	I	27	O	6	Q
32	F	6	S	12	W

Riddle
Answer: " ___ ___ ___ ___ ___ ___   ___ ___   ___ ___ ?"
             4 **8** **5** **9** **1** **7**   **10** **2**   **6** **3**

Copyright © Scholastic Inc.

Jack's Beanstalk

Name _____   Date _____

Jack's class was growing bean plants. After 1 week, Jack's was the tallest.
Measure Jack's plant below. Record its height: _____
After 2 weeks, Jack's plant had doubled in height.
How tall was it now? _____

Draw a picture to show how tall the plant grew.
Measure your drawing to make sure it is the correct height.

2 weeks.

After 3 weeks, Jack's plant was still growing!
How tall would it be now? _____
Explain your answer. _____

_____

Candy Boxes

Name _____ Date _____

Steve works in a candy store. He puts candy into boxes. Each box has 10 spaces. Steve has 32 candies. Try to draw 32 candies in the boxes below. Write the number of candies in each box on the line. Write the number of any leftover candy at the bottom of the page.

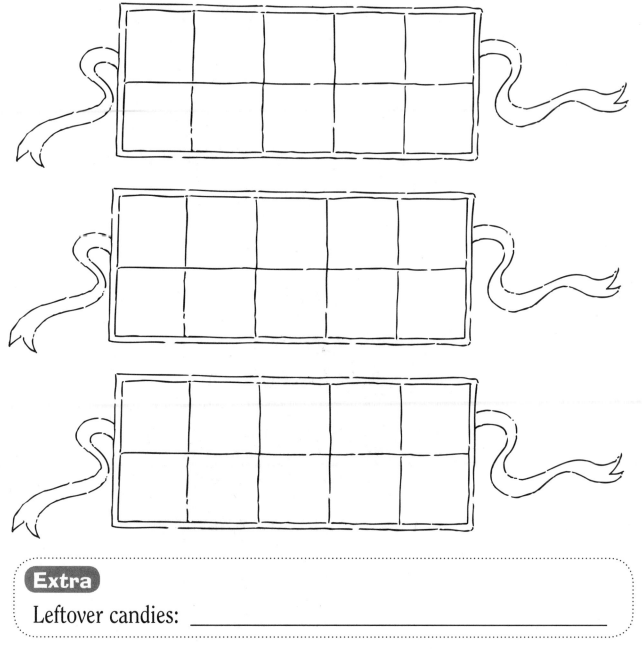

Extra

Leftover candies: _____

Copyright © Scholastic Inc.

Creature Categories

Name _____ Date _____

Nick's class took a field trip to the beach. When they looked in the tide pools, they saw a lot of animals. Group the animals they saw. Color the animals in each group the same color.

Write a word or phrase that explains how you grouped them.

Group #1 _____

Group #2 _____

Group #3 _____

Coin-Toss Addition

Name _____ Date _____

Toss 8 coins. Write "H" for heads or "T" for tails in the circles below to show your toss. Then write the addition equation. Write the number of "heads" first. We did the first one for you. Try it three times.

(H) (H) (H) (H) (T) (T) (T) (T)

Equation: _____ **4 + 4 = 8** _____

◯ ◯ ◯ ◯ ◯ ◯ ◯ ◯

Equation: _____

◯ ◯ ◯ ◯ ◯ ◯ ◯ ◯

Equation: _____

◯ ◯ ◯ ◯ ◯ ◯ ◯ ◯

Equation: _____

Copyright © Scholastic Inc.

41

Clear Reader

Name _____   Date _____

Write each sentence using numbers and symbols.

1. Four plus five is nine.	
2. Eleven minus six is five.	
3. Nine plus seven is sixteen.	
4. Four plus eight is twelve.	
5. Three minus two is one.	
6. Seven plus seven is fourteen.	
7. Fifteen minus ten is five.	
8. Two plus eight is ten.	
9. Five minus two is three.	

Flower Problems

Name _____ Date _____

Solve these story problems. Cut out the flowers at the bottom of the
page to help you.

1. Jared had a flowerpot with 7 flowers.
   He replanted 5 flowers outdoors. How
   many flowers were left in the pot?

   _____

2. Kristin planted 7 flowers.
   1 flower wilted. How many flowers were not wilted?

   _____

3. Hannah picked flowers for her father.
   She picked 3 flowers from the front yard.
   She picked 4 flowers from the back yard.
   She put them in a flowerpot.
   How many flowers did Hannah pick?

   _____

Copyright © Scholastic Inc.

Pizza Party

Name _____ Date _____

Garth's class is having a pizza party. They made a diagram to show which pizzas they would like. Draw an X in each circle to show how many classmates wanted each kind of pizza.

- 5 wanted cheese pizza.
- 10 wanted pepperoni pizza.
- 3 wanted sausage pizza.
- 2 wanted both cheese and pepperoni pizza.

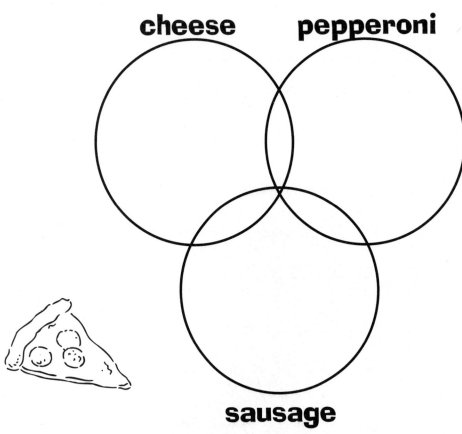

What can you learn by looking at this diagram? Write your ideas:

_____

_____

Prime Timer

Name _____ Date _____

Write the time 3 ways.

example: 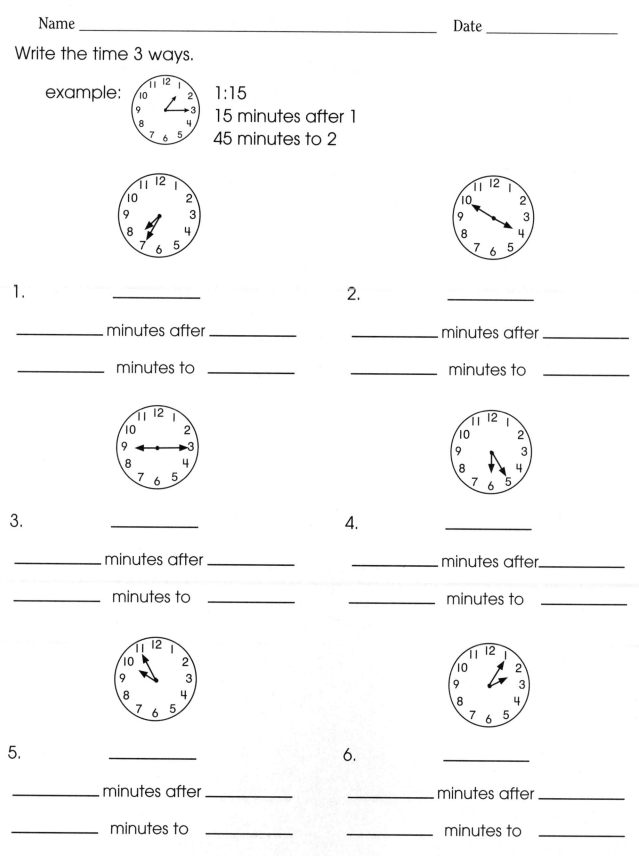 1:15
15 minutes after 1
45 minutes to 2

1. _____

_____ minutes after _____

_____ minutes to _____

2. _____

_____ minutes after _____

_____ minutes to _____

3. _____

_____ minutes after _____

_____ minutes to _____

4. _____

_____ minutes after _____

_____ minutes to _____

5. _____

_____ minutes after _____

_____ minutes to _____

6. _____

_____ minutes after _____

_____ minutes to _____

Copyright © Scholastic Inc.

Just Snacks

Name _____ Date _____

Use the menu on page 47 to answer the following questions.

1. Which snack costs the most?

   _____

   How much do they cost?

   _____

2. Which sweet costs the least? _____

   How much does it cost? _____

3. Henry spends 50¢ on a snack.
   What does he buy? _____

4. Gina orders a drink. She spends 15¢.
   Which drink does she order? _____

5. Dan orders popcorn and a cookie.
   How much does he pay? _____

6. Pat buys a cup of soup and a sip of milk.
   How much does she spend? _____

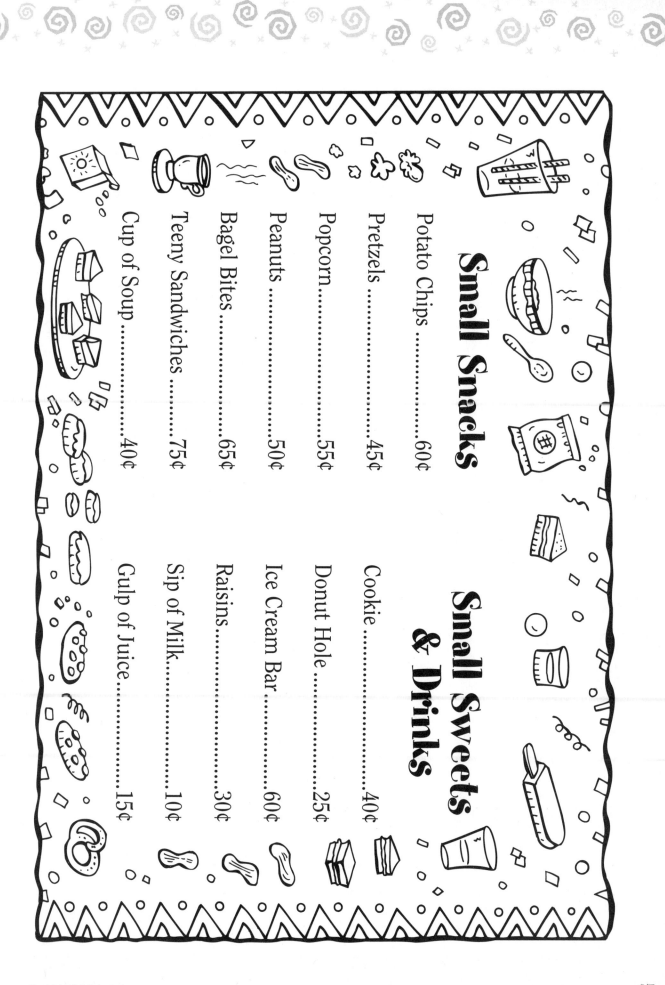

Small Snacks

Potato Chips .... 60¢

Pretzels .... 45¢

Popcorn .... 55¢

Peanuts .... 50¢

Bagel Bites .... 65¢

Teeny Sandwiches .... 75¢

Cup of Soup .... 40¢

Small Sweets & Drinks

Cookie .... 40¢

Donut Hole .... 25¢

Ice Cream Bar .... 60¢

Raisins .... 30¢

Sip of Milk .... 10¢

Gulp of Juice .... 15¢

Copyright © Scholastic Inc.

Money Matters

Name_____ Date _____

Alex asked his little brother Billy to trade piggy banks.

Alex's bank has these coins: Billy's has these coins:

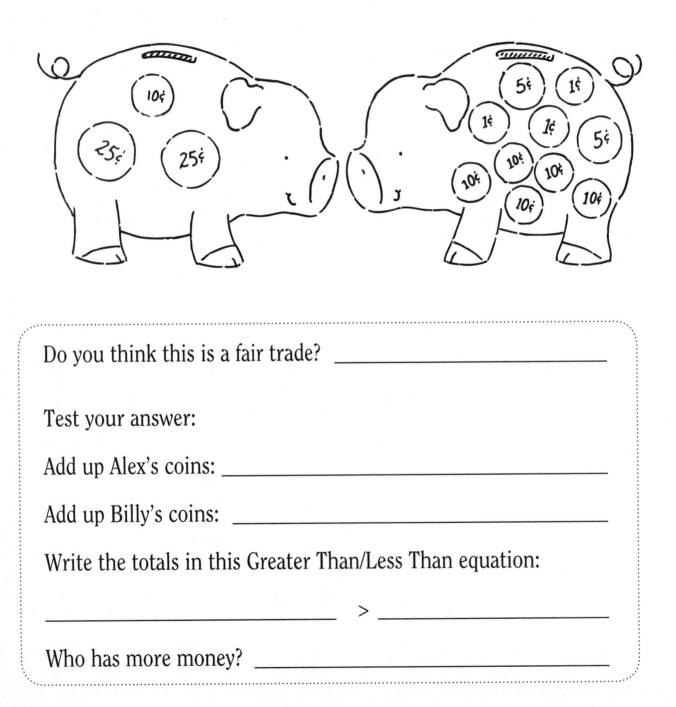

Do you think this is a fair trade? _____

Test your answer:

Add up Alex's coins: _____

Add up Billy's coins: _____

Write the totals in this Greater Than/Less Than equation:

_____ > _____

Who has more money? _____

Best Estimator

Name_____ Date _____

LENGTH CAN BE MEASURED IN INCHES (IN.), FEET (FT.), YARDS (YD.), AND MILES (MI.). 12 IN. = 1 FT. 5280 FT. = 1 MILE.

UNDERLINE THE MORE SENSIBLE MEASURE.

How many inches to Boston, Sir?

BUS STOP

7. LENGTH OF A FOOTBALL FIELD
   INCHES   YARDS

8. DISTANCE FROM EARTH TO MOON
   MILES   YARDS

9. DEPTH OF A SWIMMING POOL
   FEET   INCHES

1. HEIGHT OF A BOOKCASE
   INCHES   FEET

10. TUBE OF TOOTHPASTE
    INCHES   FEET

2. WIDTH OF YOUR BACKYARD
   YARDS   MILES

11. HEIGHT OF A REFRIGERATOR
    INCHES   FEET

3. LENGTH OF A RIVER
   MILES   YARDS

12. WIDTH OF A BEDROOM
    FEET   INCHES

4. WIDTH OF A DESK
   INCHES   FEET

13. DISTANCE BETWEEN 2 CITIES
    YARDS   MILES

5. LENGTH OF YOUR ARM
   FEET   INCHES

14. LENGTH OF A DOLLAR
    INCHES   FEET

6. LENGTH OF A COMB
   INCHES   FEET

15. LENGTH OF AN AUTOMOBILE
    INCHES   FEET

Copyright © Scholastic Inc.

Zoo Weigh-In

Name _____ Date _____

Zoey's class went to the zoo. They wrote down how much the animals weighed. Cut out the animals below. Arrange them in weight order— from lightest to heaviest.

329 lbs

358 lbs.

224 lbs.

532 lbs.

Measuring Perimeter

Name _____ Date _____

Use the inch side of a ruler and measure each side of each triangle. Write the inches in the spaces below. Then add up all the sides to find the perimeter, or distance around each triangle.

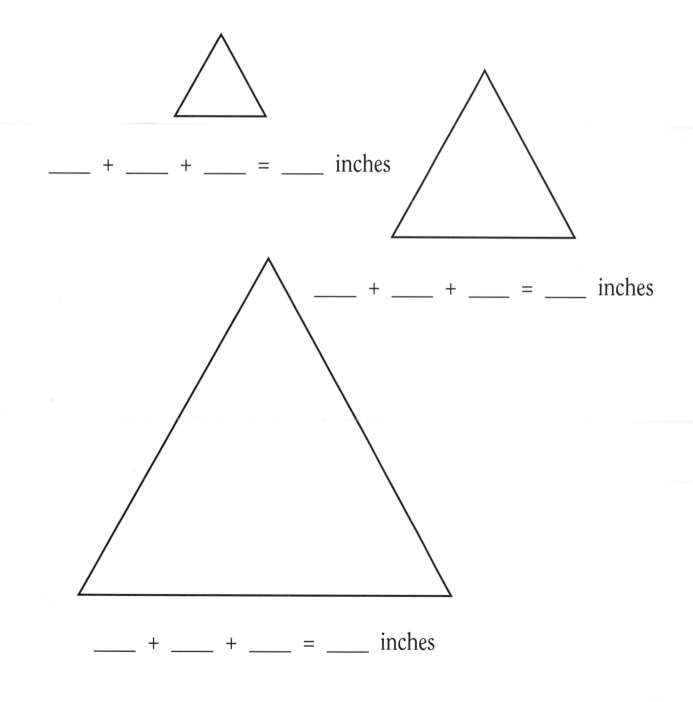

___ + ___ + ___ = ___ inches

___ + ___ + ___ = ___ inches

___ + ___ + ___ = ___ inches

Copyright © Scholastic Inc.

Night-Light

Name _____ Date _____

1. Find each number pair on the graph. Make a dot for each.

2. Connect the dots in the order that you make them.

3. What picture did you make?

_____

	Across	Up
1.	6	11
2.	5	7
3.	1	7
4.	4	5
5.	3	0
6.	6	3
7.	9	0
8.	8	5
9.	11	7
10.	7	7
11.	6	11

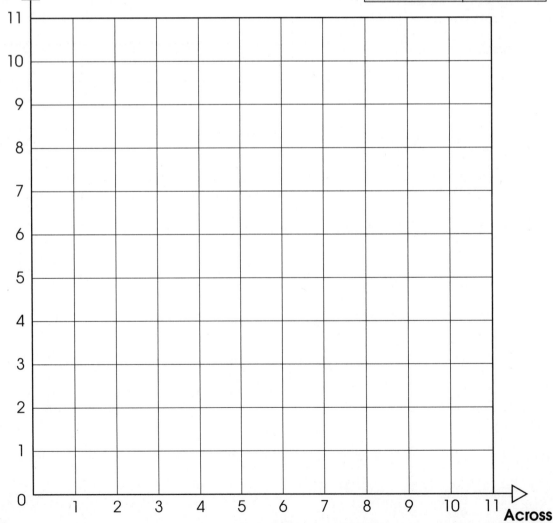

Great Graphing

Name _____ Date _____

The picture was made with 7 different shapes. How many of each shape was used? Color in the shapes, following the instructions. Then color in the boxes on the chart, 1 box for each shape used.

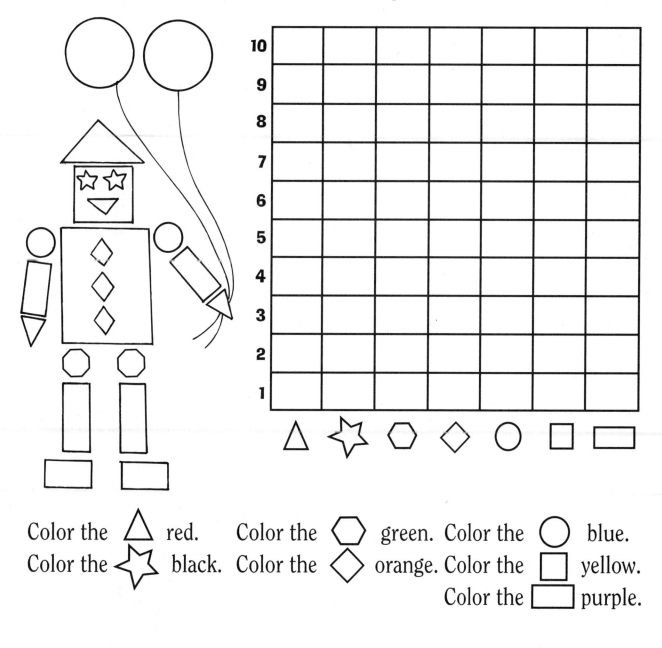

Color the △ red.　Color the ⬡ green.　Color the ○ blue.
Color the ☆ black.　Color the ◇ orange.　Color the □ yellow.
　　　　　　　　　　　　　　　　　　　Color the ▭ purple.

Which shape was used the most? _____

Copyright © Scholastic Inc.

Fruit Graph

Name _____ Date _____

Ask 12 friends which of these four fruits they like most. Fill in the graph to find out. Color one box on the graph for each vote.

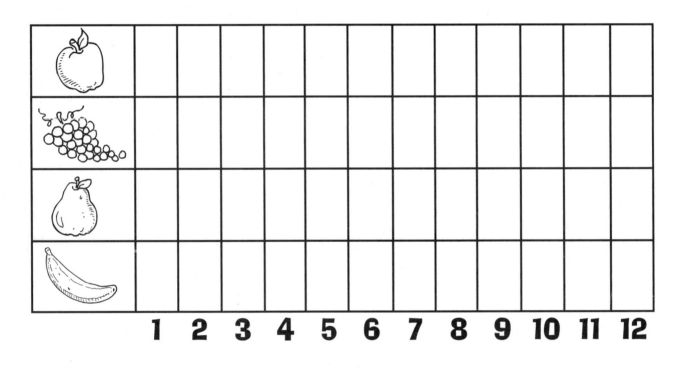

Which fruit was the most popular? _____
How many votes did it get? _____

Which fruit was the least popular? _____
How many votes did it get? _____

If two fruits got the same amount of votes, they "tied." Write any ties below.

_____ and _____

_____ and _____

Chester's Cakes and Pies

Name _____ Date _____

Fill in the blanks. Chester Chipmunk was cutting cakes and pies.
Bobby Bear said, "Some aren't cut in half. When you cut something in
half, there are _____ pieces and both of the pieces are the
same _____."

Here is how Chester cut the cakes and pies.

Circle the desserts that are cut in half correctly.

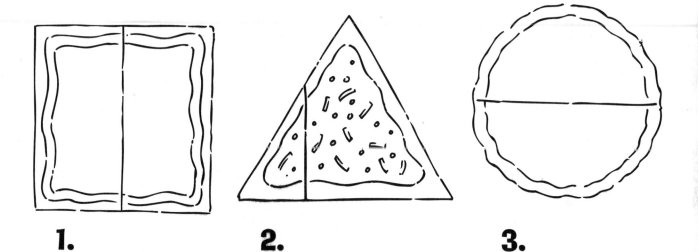

1.   **2.**   **3.**

   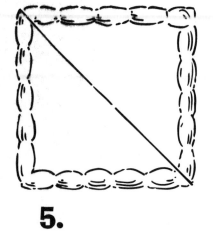   

4.   **5.**   **6.**

Copyright © Scholastic Inc.

55

Part Timer

Name _____ Date _____

Determine fractions of a whole. Check √ your answers.

1. HOW MUCH JUICE IS LEFT?

$\frac{1}{2}$
$\frac{1}{4}$
$\frac{1}{3}$

2. HOW MUCH PIZZA IS GONE?

$\frac{1}{2}$
$\frac{1}{3}$
$\frac{1}{8}$

3. HOW MUCH HAS BEEN EATEN?

$\frac{1}{3}$
$\frac{1}{6}$
$\frac{1}{4}$

4. HOW MUCH IS GONE?

$\frac{1}{4}$
$\frac{1}{2}$
$\frac{1}{8}$

5. HOW MUCH IS LACED?

$\frac{1}{2}$
$\frac{1}{3}$
$\frac{1}{4}$

6. HOW MUCH TONIC IS LEFT?

$\frac{1}{6}$
$\frac{1}{4}$
$\frac{1}{3}$

7. HOW MUCH WATER IS LEFT?

$\frac{3}{4}$
$\frac{1}{2}$
$\frac{1}{4}$

8. HOW MUCH HAS BEEN CUT OFF?

$\frac{1}{2}$
$\frac{1}{4}$
$\frac{1}{3}$

9. HOW MUCH WATER REMAINS?

$\frac{3}{4}$
$\frac{1}{2}$
$\frac{1}{4}$

10. HOW MUCH LEAF HAS BEEN EATEN?

$\frac{1}{4}$
$\frac{1}{6}$
$\frac{2}{3}$

11. HOW MUCH BREAD IS UNCUT?

$\frac{1}{4}$
$\frac{1}{3}$
$\frac{1}{2}$

Fraction Fun

Name _____ Date _____

Something that is split in 2 equal parts is divided in "half."

These two shapes are divided in half.

A fraction has a number on the top: ⟶ **1**

A fraction has a number on the bottom, too: ⟶ **2**

The top number tells the "fraction," or parts, of the whole.

The bottom number tells the number of parts in the whole.

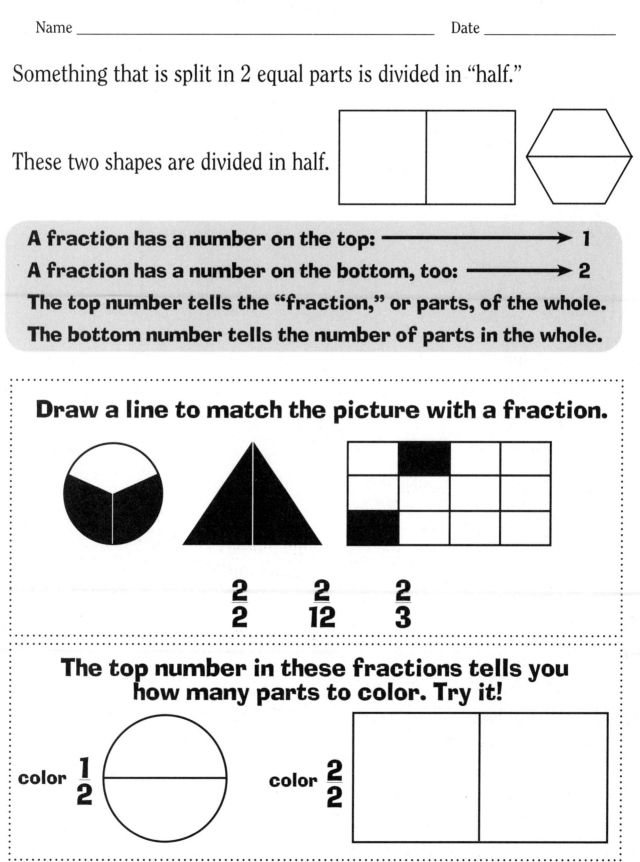

Draw a line to match the picture with a fraction.

$\dfrac{2}{2}$ $\dfrac{2}{12}$ $\dfrac{2}{3}$

The top number in these fractions tells you how many parts to color. Try it!

color $\dfrac{1}{2}$ color $\dfrac{2}{2}$

Copyright © Scholastic Inc.

Fun With Fractions

Name_____ Date _____

A fraction has two numbers. The top number will tell you how many parts to color. The bottom number tells you how many parts there are.

Color 1/5 of the circle.

Color 4/5 of the rectangle.

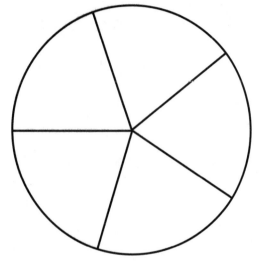

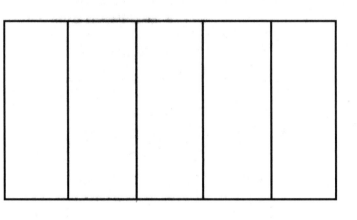

Color 3/5 of the ants.

Color 2/5 of the spiders.

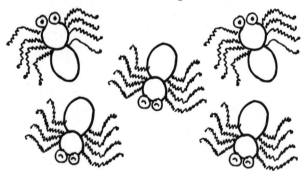

Color 0/5 of the bees.

Color 5/5 of the worms.

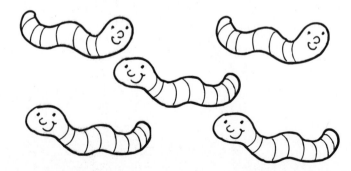

More Fun With Fractions

Name _____ Date _____

A fraction has two numbers. The top number will tell you how many parts to color. The bottom number tells you how many total parts there are.

$\frac{10}{10}$ is the whole circle.

Color $\frac{8}{10}$ of the circle.

How much is not colored? ____

$\frac{10}{10}$ is the whole rectangle.

Color $\frac{4}{10}$ of the rectangle.

How much is not colored? ____

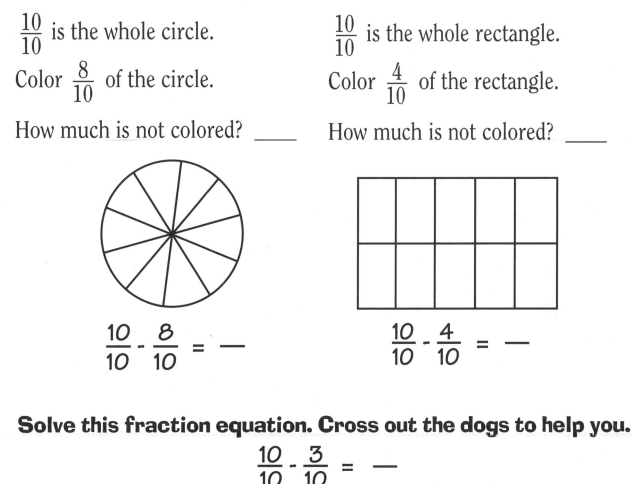

$$\frac{10}{10} - \frac{8}{10} = \underline{}$$

$$\frac{10}{10} - \frac{4}{10} = \underline{}$$

Solve this fraction equation. Cross out the dogs to help you.

$$\frac{10}{10} - \frac{3}{10} = \underline{}$$

Copyright © Scholastic Inc.

Answer Key

Page 5

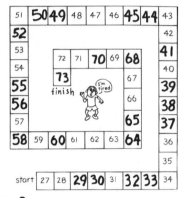

Page 6
A salamander

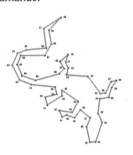

Page 7
1. 67; **2.** 34, 35; **3.** 42, 43; **4.** 16, 18
5. 73, 74, 75; **6.** 31, 32; **7.** 10 12 14 16
8. 15 18 21 24; **9.** 83, 84, 85, 86, 87, 88
10. after; **11.** before; **12.** after
13. before; **14.** before; **15.** before

Page 8
Students should follow these numbers:
13, 7, 3, 9, 19, 23, 11, 5, 17, 67, 33, 25,
27, 35, 39, 37, 23, 57, 47, 43, 21, 15, 39, 29

Page 9
Top side of the street: 52, 56
Bottom side of the street: 53, 55
Extra: The even numbers are on one side of the street.
The odd numbers are on the other side of the street.

Page 10
1. the 1st **2.** the 16th **3.** James Buchanan
4. Andrew Johnson **5.** 14

Page 11
1. 11 < 21; **2.** 56 < 72; **3.** 47 = 47; **4.** 64 >10
5. 59 = 59; **6.** 38 >17; **7.** 526 < 527; **8.** 159 > 42
9–16. Answers will vary. **17.** 73 61 54 37
18. 96 43 24 22; **19.** 79 78 69 51
20. 51 37 27 15

Page 12
A sidewalk.
518, 315, 276, 693, 137, 564, 909, 811, 209, 717, 836, 321,
488, 857, 432, 707

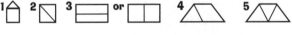

Page 13

324, 435, 546, **657, 768, 879**

□ O △ □ O △ □ O △

ㅋ ㅌ ㅋ ㅌ ㅋㅌㅋㅋ

□□ ☑ □ □ ☑ □ ☑ □□

ACEGIK MOQSU

11:05, 11:10, 11:15, **11:20, 11:25**

Page 14
1 ⌂ 2 ◫ 3 ▭ **or** ⊟ 4 ▱ 5 ◿◺

This line   This line
could move   could move
up or down.   left or right.

Page 15
1. 32, 42, 52, 62, 72, 82, 92
2. 70, 60, 50, 40, 30, 20, 10
3. 67, 57, 47, 37, 27, 17, 7
4. 44, 55, 66, 77, 88, 99

Page 16
Answers will vary.

Page 17
A. 1. F, **2.** G, **3.** B, **4.** C or A, **5.** E, **6.** I, **7.** E, **8.** H, **9.** G,
10. G, **11.** C; **B. 1.** B, **2.** F, **3.** D, **4.** I, **5.** F, **6.** E, **7.** A, **8.** D, **9.**
I, **10.** F, **11.** I; **C. 1.** I, **2.** C, **3.** C, **4.** G, **5.** G, **6.** C, **7.** F, **8.** I,
9. B, **10.** C or A, **11.** F

Page 18
Beans talk
4 + 2 = 6; 7 + 7 = 14; 9 + 5 = 14; 10 + 4 = 14;
4 + 8 = 12; 6 + 8 = 14; 11 + 3 = 14; 14 + 0 = 14;
7 + 2 = 9; 13 + 1 = 14; 5 + 8 = 13; 12 + 2 = 14;
7 + 4 = 11; 5 + 9 = 14